World Stage Press
Verse from the Village

FORMIDABLE SHADOWS
A FOSTER YOUTH JOURNEY

FORMIDABLE SHADOWS
A FOSTER YOUTH JOURNEY

AC THE POET

World Stage Press
Verse from the Village

World Stage Press
Verse from the Village

Formidable Shadows: A Foster Youth Journey
© 2024 AC the Poet
ISBN: 978-1-952952-62-3

Cover Image © 2023 Adam Martinez

First Edition, 2024

All rights reserved. No part of this publication may be reproduced, distributed, or transmitted in any form or by any means, including photocopying, recording, or other electronic or mechanical methods, without the prior written permission of the publisher, except in the case of brief quotations embodied in critical reviews and certain other noncommercial uses permitted by copyright law.

Printed in the United States of America

Edited by Kiana Shaley Martin & Ruddy Lopez
Cover Design by Adam Martinez & Emily Anne Evans
Layout Design by Krystle May Statler & Emily Anne Evans

This collection is dedicated to any youth or adult who is struggling on their journey, no matter what part of the journey they are on.

This is especially dedicated to anyone who has had experience in the foster care system, LGBTQI+ folx, and all the immigrant and undocumented souls.

*It's for anyone who has ever felt unseen, lost or not part of this universe.
A reminder that it is okay to feel through all the feelings and express them.*

*I hope you find a space that resonates and relates to you through these pages.
It's been a difficult journey but every step has brought me here.*

"Some things can only be seen in the shadows."

Carlos Ruiz Zafón

Contents

Preface   xv

I. ROOT SHADOWS
Generational Garden	5
Dawn Rises	6
Phasing Through Water	9
The Countdown	10
Thoughts	13

II. MOTHER SHADOW
Pepperoni Explosion	17
Raised by Unhealed Trauma:	18
Mirage Mirror	19
How to Feed a Narcissist	20
Replay	21
Drunk Driving	23
Thoughts II	

III. FATHER SHADOW   24
Grateful I Never Grew a Tail	27
I miss you, childhood.	28
Our Father, Hallowed Be Thy Name	29
Letter to Sobriety	30
Through the Ages: 0-32	32

Thoughts III	35
Where Is love?	36

IV. REFRACTED REPLACEMENTS

Condescending Apologies	39
I Gotta Go Potty…	41
Uncle Frankie	43
Teachings from Tío	44
La Tóxica (Yo)	45
To Kiss Her	47
Revolving Compass	48

V. SHADOW SELF

Formidable Shadows	53
PTSD Love	54
I am Permanently in Foster Care	56
I am a Temporary Home	57
Effervescent	58
Coming Out	60
Metaverse Brain	61
Ventriloquist Song	62
1000 Photographs	63
Orlando	65
Coworker	67
Singed Piña	68
2021 Masquerade	70
Cortisol Addiction	72
Nightmares	73
Water is a Universal Language	75
Rooted Canal	78

VI. EMBRACING THE LIGHT

Status 1	81
Status 2	81
Status 3	81
Status 4	81
Status 5	81
Synchronized Divination	82
Utility Poles Stay Stagnant	83
Healing Cells	84
Be-longing.	86
Illusion of Choice	87
Dissecting the Insect	89
A 40-year Contract	90
Imperfect Pictures	91
Fell in Love with Perfect Imperfection	92
Hiding Shadows	94
Indisposable	95
The Designer	96
The Shadow Waved and I Finally Recognized It	97

Acknowledgments   99

Preface

This book is a long time coming, a compilation of my journey from when I began performing at open mics and expressing my life and myself on stage. As a reader, you will find poetry on mental health struggles from the lowest parts of depression to coming into my identities. You'll explore poems about my family and being in the foster care system, others on my adopted family and the death of loved ones. Toward the end of the book, you'll even find some poems leaning into the healing part of my journey—most of those poems have been left out as another book is coming out (of the closet) that will showcase more of my healing process.

Formidable Shadows releases the deepest pains of a traumatic childhood using writing as a healing process. Poetry was my form of release through radical truth-telling, an expression of my inner tribulations and hardships. As you explore the pages, I hope you reflect on your own life and notice what resonates and what doesn't. Maybe there is someone in your own life walking a similar path or maybe you have had a similar experience. As you reflect, my hope is that you find space in your soul to breathe in what you needed then, so you can take care of your own inner child now. *Formidable Shadows* releases the deepest pains and hurts of a childhood, bringing healing into adulthood in the form of poetry. This book expresses an older version of myself that's been held onto for longer than desired (eleven years).

As you go through my life story, another hope is that you are inspired to write or speak your own truth—wherever you are in your process. Writing can support you in getting thoughts and feelings out of your mind, body and soul to process and feel through the emotions and experiences. Writing saved me from myself and others. It kept me grounded and safe. Safety became my priority in life as I didn't have it growing up.

Thank you again for purchasing this first compilation of my *Formidable Shadows*. You reading this sheds light into each shadow and reveals the love that is needed to be seen. You are now a part of my story. This is only the beginning. There's a lifetime of healing, love and growth ahead.

FORMIDABLE SHADOWS

I. ROOT SHADOWS

Generational Garden

You / the 30-year-old me / interrupt my bath as I pour the jug of nuked water on my sprouting head / I am seven / cleansing impurities from unhealed wounds / freezer burn from frostbit family treaties / winter / has brought the annual polar vortex / and pipes are icicles again / each year / I imagine the icicles / relics that transport / to warmer realities / truth is / life has never been at a comfortable temperature.

You / the 30-year-old me / bring a soapy washcloth / Band-Aids and warm / gentle hands that / scrub off lingering of screams / and vulgarities / I'm naked / and comfortable / as I pick up the bucket / microwaved water that / mother prepared for me.

Mother / handed me the jug with cold calluses / and dirt from the garden / Mother / feels like ice cream on a -10 degree day / I'm still too young / to understand poverty / but I do understand temperature / I take the bucket of tears / cleanse the open wounds / hoping the salt sanitizes / before infection.

You / the 30-year-old me / bring a steamy towel / fresh clothes / and offer to brush / tangles of trauma from my scalp / I don't mind my roots / brushed now / I get to spend / more time in your sun / I feel fertilizer feeding / nutrients with every laugh / hug from your rays / can't wait to bloom into you / one day.

Dawn Rises
For my adopted mom, Dawn

Seeing the world after a cancer diagnosis…

Everything is infected…the leaves have lost their luster.
I used to see their color changing as intrinsic,
as significant…now they are diseased.
The brown has metastasized into each vein.

The sun no longer smiles at the awakening of the world.
It stays behind…sleeps in,
too weary to get out of bed.

The earth is poisoned…
I breathe her air but it's full of smog…
the water…only drowns.
My face is fake
painted happiness
a clown mask of illusion.
I'm living but not really alive.

Feel the pain they say…
and I do…hidden behind closed doors…
cracked only enough to let some of the cancer in…
as it slowly destroys…

Eventually, I will learn to get out of bed,
my heart will not weigh me down…
but I dread that day…
so I remind myself of what's not cancer.
Her smile, the stubborn
and compassionate way she reminds us of her existence.

Her laugh, the way she calls me kiddo
and has allowed me to be a part of her family.
Her strength...
even now as cancer taints her beauty...
She rises, she laughs and she hugs.

Enter **Stage 4**, like this is a performance and each stage has an
act with an audience...
The applause is heard through the word.

Chemotherapy.
Che...**mo** • **ther** • a...py.

I want to give her my liver.
My lungs.
My bones.
My brain.
Everything that's not cancer.
Free from all the attacks
free from performances
filled with health...filled with safety.
Stage 5.

I...
found out there is a stage 5 after the doctor said there was an
80% chance of her pulling through...
and then 3 weeks later...
stage 4 metastasized.

Stage 5
is when cancer has taken over the physical body.
that phone call I was dreading...
it's funeral.
It's pretending everything is okay,
it's trying to paint on face...
and not having enough make-up...

Everything has turned cold.
Leaves have turned to snow…
I used to see winter as beautiful,
the wind whispering clouds to the trees,
icicles as glistening handles into new realms.
Now it is desolate, a desert storm of emotions,
it's glacial titanic, heart sinking into a somber depression.
I'm in a chronic heart attack that never goes away…

and slowly entering stage 6…

Stage 6 is complicated
It's tears streaming through Spotify and then wiping with a napkin.
It's inability to focus, it's being behind, fallen scraped knees
and then climbing back up.

Stage 6 is remission…
it's resiliency and I'm remembering what it looks like.

No matter what cancer does,
she will always to me…be cancer-free.

Even as the leaves change. As the snow accumulates.

The sun still rises and Dawn is here.
Mom is still here.

Phasing Through Water

They flow as water does, with memory.
Pure but must be protected as pollution easily permeates.
They are love in the softest ways—a sandy shore, a small pour.
They are growing, a transcending river carving canyons.
And they have all the time they need to be at each stage.
From the raindrop to the puddle __
The lake to the ocean _____
And even as a vapor { }
A cloud unseen until condensation accumulates and they flow…
Down the drain.
A lingering pain, letting grow to another day.
They flow, as water does, with memory.

The Countdown

I am 8 years old.
And writing my first suicide letter.
Age 8, I want to die.
Find that life is too difficult and wish for a time machine.
Shaking pen hand, trembling my goodbyes, across red construction paper.
Shouting silence to the world
I don't belong, never belonged.
Tears, smudging letters, creating thumbprints, evidence of my existence.
Existence I want to wash away.

Moments flood the mind,
moments alone at this table with thoughts and a pen.
As a child, I watch my family drown themselves
with poison and addiction so they don't have to feel any longer.
Everyone is slowly taking their lives
so I decided to write away mine.

Age 14, I take razor blades to my arms to cut the hurt off,
trying to get rid of the evidence of my failures.
I take scissors to my legs and stomach
to become smaller.
Shaking scissors interlaced in defiant fingers,
cutting off memories, ridding my body of ugly,
of laughing, pointing children mooing in the hallway.
Hoping to be my own lipo-surgeon.

Age 15, I find my uncle's suicide letter,
written on canvas so elegantly.
Telling everyone it wasn't their fault
and not to blame themselves.
I spend hours at my uncle's grave,
contemplating why, justifying his reasons, then justifying mine.

I imagine his moment,
staring down the black hole barrel of a gun,
the smell of dumpster death lingering,
contemplating the moments that came to this.
Counting the bullets in the chamber,
1, 2, 3...
Each a different tragedy leading to this.
One click into position,
raise the black hole where an outstretched hand should be—
a heart should be.
He goes unnoticed, like the silence of a tree
in the woods that nobody hears.

With one click.
I always dream of how we would both be happy when we meet in
spirit,
I'll fly through the clouds and greet him with a smile.
Letting him know that our kind
are too great for the physical world.

At 23, I wrap a belt around my neck,
the belt, to end the nuisance of breathing.
I pull, playing tug of war with my breath.
Before collapsing to the floor
and clutching the dying inside me.
Wheezing in and out of a self-induced asthma attack.
Each belt notch marking a tragedy,
a devastating memory coming to where the belt loop meets the strap.

Age 25, I learned that my brother drove his truck at a tree.
Key burning in ignition, foot on the pedal
revving the engine to life.
He never felt so alive.
Shifter in park,
just three shifts down.
1, 2, 3
and the moment of adrenaline,
the moment of impact.
Fingers caress the button,
contemplating the moments
Three shifts down.
1, 2, 3
Engine charging ahead,
tree in sight as he closes his eyes.

My brother wouldn't be here
if he hadn't gotten stuck in the mud
right before the crash.
That's when I stopped dreaming
of my own death,
when I realized that someone
I loved and cared about
was dreaming of theirs.

Thoughts

No one cares about me.

I am worthless.

No one desires me.

My only use is to be used.

I don't have power.

I'm useless.

I'm not smart.

I'm lazy.

I can't focus.

I'm unlovable.

I don't matter.

I don't belong anywhere.

No one loves me.

I hate myself.

I can't do anything right.

Why am I even here?

No one cares. No one cares. No one cares. No one cares.
No one cares. No-one—
I don't care.

You taught me to be cold, frozen was the only way to keep my shape.

Sturdy.
Nothing gets in, nothing gets out.
Be stoic. Survive.
You never let me in. So all I became was warm.
Flowing into other vessels. Parts of me combining with theirs.
Fluid. No boundaries.
I learned to sink into the dirtiest soil.
My soul surfacing slightly stained.
And now
I balance on both.
Resembling the plasma of the sun
And each crater of the moon.
I wander as a star.
In-between.
Unsure how many light-years ago I died.

II. MOTHER SHADOW

Pepperoni Explosion

My mother is like pepperoni pizza rolls forgotten in the microwave.
The insides being too hot and too cold and spewed all over the plate.
She's never at the right temperature no matter the weather,
And loving her is like driving on the freeway during rush hour in a blizzard—
It's dangerous with inevitable outcomes,
Yet I still do it.

Even when it's only about her—
When her depression pulls me into demons and swallows me like Jonah's whale.
It usually happens around my birthday
After I ask for too many hugs,
And she's been double-fisting whiskey and chasing beer.

That's when the insides get too hot,
When they explode all over, searing my skin.
One time she blamed me for wanting to die.
Another, she just hated my existence.
As I heal, I learn that she just hates herself.
That I am a mirror reflecting her own self-worth back at her.

And she can't contain the pain,
So she has to shatter the mirror.
It's the only way she knows to be okay.
So I've learned the only way to save the mirror, to save myself,
Is really just to stay away
And polish my own reflection.

Raised by Unhealed Trauma:

No one taught me how to make my bed.
No one taught me how to iron my clothes.
No one taught me how to cook nutritious meals.
No one taught me how to communicate my thoughts and feelings.
No one taught me how to love others appropriately.
No one taught me how to regulate my emotions.
No one taught me how to take care of my desires.
No one taught me about my journey.
No one taught me how to express my identity.
No one taught me about protecting myself.
No one taught me how to consent.
No one taught me about boundaries.
No one taught me the physical signs of being uncomfortable.
No one taught me. They didn't know themselves.

I taught myself.

Mirage Mirror

What if the moon
is a mirror and a
reflection of how the sun sees
itself at night?
And the stars are tiny fragments of
refracted glass, shattered thoughts
of unworthiness. And if this is true,
then there are phases
and even times when
the mirror disappears.
Let the mirror
disappear.
Just let the mirror
disappear.

How to Feed a Narcissist

Bake your insecurities into homemade bread
Your worries into the finest fruit pie
Shower narcissist in confetti and glitter
Everywhere they walk is grand entry, red carpet.
Give compliments like candy
Beg them to stay over and over
Show them your vulnerabilities
Let them get close
Cry when they touch you
Apologize even when it was their fault lines that were trembling
Become the moon and name them Earth
Allow your moon to revolve around them constantly
Place them in the middle of your dining room table
They are the centerpiece for every occasion
Be the tree that exhales their oxygen to breathe
Let them cut you down and turn you into a step stool
Lift them above your branches
Give all of your warmth until your heart
Gets so cold they need to throw the step stool into the fire to keep warm
And you become thick smoke
So thick that they can't breathe you anymore
And they suffocate.

Replay

Cyclical cycles, repeating repetition, record skipping—
record skipping
Ski-ski-skippingggg
I found myself at the beginning again. In the same track on replay
Old patterns, outdated energy
But this time I stood tall, I recognized it.

Did my best to avoid her, avoid her
Got so good at no contact
Apparently, distance does make the heart grow fonder
Cuz she kept coming back
Couldn't take a hint
She wasn't listening
And I was hardly talking
Difficult to hold conversation
Felt the guilt squeeze my throat every time
I wanted to interrupt with...
You're toxic. You're toxic.

But my tongue wouldn't let me
my tastebuds translating to something more palpable
Like I don't really want to go out tonight and I'm busy
Keeping that door open
And she kept knock-ing, knock-ing,
Like knock-knock who's there?
I became the punch line in my own joke
What I needed to say was you remind me of my narcissistic alcoholic mother
And I don't really wanna be your DD again, again.

I've learned
The way to train a narcissist
Is not to feed them.

They start to see you as the problem
They start to question if you belong in their life
And so I kept protecting my energy
Stood within my boundaries
          And the track finally went to the next song.

Drunk Driving

I'm the DD tonight / for real / not just the DD for the moment while I sip on this mixed drink and take a shot / You're a DD too I heard / a Drunk Driver / and I don't mean to make ya feel bad / I've seen too many DDs/ become DBs / Dead Bodies / and too many I'll be okays / become unlicensed the next day / I don't want to ruin your mood / but my mom alone / could drink you all under the table / and be the best DD here / but three DUIs later / and she still hasn't learned / I guess we all / have our methods / self-prescribed medication / that gets us through / the pain / I've watched alcohol / turn my Halloween costume / into reality / called it mom / there were too many times / at the age of 9 / where I had to take / the wheel / instead of Jesus / our lives were in my hands / I knew the definition / of broken family / before I knew how / to speak / it started with alcohol / I understood / the pain of domestic violence / before feeling / any impact of a hit / because / I watched alcohol / break my mother's arm / slam her head into a mirror / I witnessed alcohol / turn the employed / into *"Sorry we're not hiring"* / I've watched it / make excuses / and turn suicidal ideations / into buried coffins / mere memories / I hated how alcohol / turned original whole beings / into recycled pieces / so before / you are the DD / for the moment / and drink your bottle / while fumbling / for your keys / ask yourself / if / you / want / to be just another / tombstone copy / of Death by DUI / and undreamt dreams.

Thoughts II

Does she love me? Does she hate me?
How do I avoid her anger? Her pain?

Why is she screaming at me?
What did I do this time?

Why am I never good enough?
Why can't I ever get it right?

I'll read in my bedroom.
All day.
Hidden.

I still love her,
Even if she doesn't love me.

What can I do to get her to love me?
How can I be enough?

I'll give her hugs on her birthday.
She doesn't want hugs.

I'll give her love every day.
She doesn't want love or attention.

I'll hide myself.
Pretend not to exist. Be quiet. Be still. Be forgotten. Be gone.
Be a shadow.

III. FATHER SHADOW

Grateful I Never Grew a Tail

Whenever he was angry
    He beat the dogs.
When my mother cheated
    He beat the dogs.
When we were beating each other
    He beat the dogs.
When he caught me stealing
    He beat the dogs.
When he wanted to teach us kids
    He beat the dogs.
When life got too difficult
    He beat the dogs.
When he had too much to drink
    He beat the dogs.
When the dogs ran out of food
    He beat the dogs.
When the heater went out
    He beat the dogs.
When the pipes froze
    He beat the dogs.
When child protection services came
    He beat the dogs.
When he didn't know what to do
    He beat the dogs.

When the dogs ran away
    He disappeared.

        —Grateful I never grew a tail.

As I grew older I came to understand emotional regulation and how he didn't have an outlet—we were all surviving.

I miss you, childhood.

I miss you, I miss that smile on your face
when daddy came home from work.
I miss your youthful laugh before the world tore you apart,
when you were too young to understand damage and hurt.
I miss when you were sleeping,
before you started having nightmares during the day.
I miss running with you on playgrounds and in the yard,
you would jump around the plants in the garden barely grazing by.
I miss climbing trees with you
and finding rollie pollies hidden under branches.
I miss playing on the swings, I even miss the bad things.
I miss the carefree way you held life and if you were still here,
my childhood, I'd always hold you tight and never let you go.

Our Father, Hallowed Be Thy Name

Our Father who isn't here
Hollowed be thy name
Thy girlfriend come and thy leave us
without any notice but blame
Give us this day, your daily time
and get to know your children
but alas you'll forget our birthdays
As you lead us to hatred and loathing
but we deliver you from responsibility
and give that to our mom
A woman.

Letter to Sobriety

Dear Magistrate,

I bet you have a father.
Maybe he was never there, casting shadow in darkness, unseen.
Maybe he left at a young age, before things became violent.
Maybe you only met his sperm, as it created you.
Maybe he was abusive.
Or maybe he nurtured you and kept you grounded.
And maybe he continues to keep you grounded.

If so, I may envy you.
My father's *"child support"* replaced his hugs.
I saw his money in place of him, I swallowed burning swords branding the distaste in my mouth in forsaken loss.
He had a drinking addiction…his father used to beat him.
He watched his father down fifths like oil spills in oceans.
The alcoholic of Atlantis.
He watched his father die at twenty from the same poison.
How that can impact a soul.
How can you cope from there?
When you are twenty… and you find something to take it all away.
And that's what he did.

Following his father's footsteps, he became the same.

Entered the cage of broken promises and regretful tattoos of liquid amnesia.

But hope was always a dove flying behind him.
He just could not see it.
My father has always been the Wikipedia of good dad.
The one you gotta double-check resources.

One thing I am grateful for...is that he still exists...
And there's a newfound chance to change our relationship.

You may see him as a third DUI, resisting arrest, driving on a suspended license and THC in his system...a loser who never had a chance.
Ya, to you it looks pretty bad...a criminal with a court-appointed defendant, can't afford representation...a hopeless case on life support...

But...in this forest fire...there's new seeds germinating.
My father has awakened...sees morning dew on fresh spring grass, and found a rebirthing of his soul.
He just hit the jackpot of lows and has a new determination.
And I see it too.

I finally have that two-hour phone conversation that every child dreams
I finally have weekly check-ins and connections being built.
I'm finally getting to know this stranger.
His hopes, his dreams and what brings him life.

He wants to be a part of mine...go to poetry shows and even perform.
We want to make YouTube videos together and inspire others.

He is changing and entering a different season and you have the power to
       -pull the-
               -plug-
-while he's still breathing.

Through the Ages: 0-32

0:
Water breaks and waves of love dance into my newborn lungs, resting at home

1:
Home catches fire to feel the warmth of love that isn't found in parental hearts

2:
Hearts are bleeding and mother bathes me in radioactive water

3:
Water nourishes with unexpected encouragement and learning

5:
Learning tight hugs from mother every time I hear screams and HE leaves

6:
Leaves are blacked out **age 4** memories and tangled in **age 7** trees of family poverty and trauma

7:
Trauma teaches fight or flight and sometimes it's best to say nothing

7:
Nothing is found in brick walls as we are taken to foster homes

8:
Homes that comfort and care as I do for my brother with rosary prayers

9:
Prayers churning hope out of air and tears to spread on burnt toast to the future

10:
Future vomiting on my black velvet dress on the first day back and Cold picks me up from school

11:
School is escape and love is physical, belt marks and bruises

12:
Bruises with no boundaries, doors unhinged, diaries read, toys thrown away

13:
Away as I run track and Cold puts love on layaway

14:
Layaway is left unpaid, abandoned and wounds hold secret love notes

15:
Notes to new love that holds open doors with hinges and tells me I'm pretty

16:
Pretty becomes permanent, branding me his for use in private bedrooms

17:
Bedrooms with uncomfortable fetishes and fantasies with unlearned boundaries

18:
Boundaries are unprotected and forgiven through words and rough hands

19:
Hands write recommendations and bring love to campus visits

20:
Visits that lead to toasty futures spread with blueberry jam

21:
Jammed notebooks with knowledge, long island iced teas and side hustles

22:
Hustling with swallowed glass from too many drinks and responsibilities

23:
Responsibilities taken abroad and swallowed by abortion pills—unforgiving regret

24:
Regret is depressed and love is laid away on a long island but still open

25:
Open mic discovery and voicing vulnerability into poetry, love is homeless but connected

26:
Connected to trauma-bonded friendships, adopted death and master decisions to leave

27:
Leave, back abroad to tropical blue water

28:
Water that nourishes with collective organizing and kind words

29:
Words that solve puzzles, answer prayers and graduate from jammed notebooks

30:
Notebooks that are being re-read and written but are still breathing

31:
Breathing and surfing on higher waves of water

32:
Water breaks and waves of love dance into my newborn lungs, resting at home

Thoughts III

Father, you call me
And all we can talk about is the weather
You strive for connection
And I'm like my mother
Cold shoulder
I have nothing to say
Nothing to give
I don't want your hugs
I don't want your love
All you talk about is football
All you care about is coins
I love the idea of you
I despise reality
You want forgiveness
I'm still bleeding on my 5th-grade dress
I'm proud of your journey
I'm more proud of mine.

Where Is love?

Where can I find it? Who can I find it from?

I wonder.

From you?

IV. REFRACTED REPLACEMENTS

Condescending Apologies

Dear Friend,

I got accepted into grad school!
I'm so excited.
I guess I'm not as excited as I should be because I only have three months to say I'm sorry, I apologize.

Three months to make amends, to take back all the words I said that slithered through your ear canal, leaving remnants of venom in your cranial cavity, acidifying your bloodstream and sucking the blood from your heart...
Leaving it colder than bitter frostbit ankles on long winter hikes through Antarctica.
I left it below freezing.

And now I have three months to thaw freezer burn, to defibrillate your heart from cardiac arrest, repair puncture wounds and warm your soul with hot cocoa.

I'm sorry that's not enough, not enough time because I caused more than three months' worth of damage and instead of healing your wounds I've been blanketing them in bleach, whitewashing them to agonizing thresholds, digging into your skin deeper and deeper beyond what any skin graft can repair.

I apologize for not being genuine, for pretending everything was Alice in Wonderland shoveling all the pain down the rabbit hole and now...Where's Alice? Searching for her in a Where's Waldo portrait. And finding that she doesn't exist, or maybe she's in disguise.

I'm sorry for sounding condescending, for drowning your tears, when I said I was proud of you, I meant it. I am so fucking proud of

you. I hope that sounded heartfelt…it was, it is.
My apologies for taking jokes too far, not understanding boundaries or understanding but still crossing the line. Every time. Treating you as a finish line in a marathon race I shouldn't have crossed. But I did. Life's not a competition but sometimes we treat it like it is.

Now I have three months to shred the sorrow on pages in your book of pain, turning them into confetti pieces thrown on your birthday.
Each becomes a wish for the future that could come true after you blow out the candles.
I wish you happiness, I wish you love. I wish you healed wounds. Scabbed over, turned to scars that I can only hope go away eventually.

You've always meant the world to me, and I still love you. Take out that piece of paper that I gave you…I still love you.
These next three months I will help craft our resentment into paper airplanes named X and O that we can fly in our spare time. Every time they crash will be the last line in a goodbye letter XOXO from me to you.

Sincerely, I hope you forgive me.
P.S. I'm sorry that I wrote this into a poem but this was my only way of knowing that you'd hear my apology.

I Gotta Go Potty...

Abuela says as I follow her to the living room at 6 am.
"Where's the potty?"

And in her accent it sounds like a party.
Like a morning fiesta.
And it is.
Every day she gets up and remembers herself.
It is.
I wonder what she is thinking and half the time I never ask.
Dismissing her thoughts as unrecognizable and disconnected.
A Rubik's Cube with too many edges that I never take my time with.

I ask, "Grandma, Grandma, what are you thinking?"
Empty stare.
Vacia.
I lean in closer and ask again.
With a different frequency of the tongue.
"Abue, abue, que piensas?"

The familiar.
Not lack of respect but to let her know she is home.
And she's home.
The final Rubik's piece locked into place.

"Mija"

"Mija, I was thinking of the little boy down the corner
They taught him to grow his nails, mija"

At this point I usually dismiss.
Wondering what ignorance will escape.
But I keep listening.
I look at her nails, long and untamed.

"…So he can scratch his face, mija
And just in case he needs them"

With a little frown.
I can tell she's concerned and frightened.
She grew up in the violence.
Like a third language.
Always searching for her identity.

"There was a pond mija,
I hope he didn't drown."

I look at her nails.
She never lets us cut them.
She's the little boy.
And I frown.

Now I see her.
Can feel each scar.
Finally, I understand why.
Why her caretaker lets her do anything she wants.
Even not in her best interest.

So she doesn't have to grow her nails any longer.
And she can just go potty.
Without drowning.
Or scratching her face.

Uncle Frankie

I first met you in high school and I still remember the pain it caused when I mentioned my brother's name, Joey. Watching your tears turn to ice, I realized what I had done. Peeling the scab of a 30-year-old wound, exposing the tissue and puncturing your soul. I'm sorry tío.

Since I didn't know you, I didn't understand that the mere mention of my—I mean your brother's name could lead you to so much pain.
Suicide doesn't end the pain, it just transfers it to others and with every transfer the pain becomes stronger.

Flash forward a few years without contact. I almost forgot your name when I finally got to meet you again. You asked to have a drink with me—I agreed not completely understanding the issue until you pulled into a self-serve car wash and walked up to a local liquor store for a quick buzz. You grabbed a 16 oz can and chugged it in a parking lot, mocking me for my full can.

Driving shortly after to another 16 oz can of buzz that was your caffeine.
That's how you survived.
That's how you covered the pain.
We then went to an alley and I watched as you drank and drank until I said stop…begged you to stop because you were opening my wound and stabbing a scab of mine deep in my soul.

I asked you not to drive mom, I asked you not to drive.
Why did you drive?
Tío, as you asked your brother why,
Why did you want to die?

Teachings from Tío

You taught me to see the picture in broken sidewalk cracks—

Peering intently into each fissure, connecting the lines.
I learned to see faces in tree bark and objects in the clouds…
Finding that everything around us tells a story, its own and one of many.
Every object has a shadow.

La Tóxica (Yo)

Kati Liliana Gatgens, *nos conocimos* under such circumstances.
I am safe now, no *tengo miedo*, I feel safe now.
To say your name Kati Liliana Gatgens
Pero no estás aquí.
A forbidden fruit cut from Adam's throat.
Allowing the world to dictate our connection with snakes.
The community had a say in how we exchanged energies.
If I could go back, I would be the rose I needed
So that you could be the *rosa* you needed
And we could cultivate our garden together.
With protection.
You were always so good at being yourself.
Entering a room with *confianza*
Sitting on my toilet, door open, smoking your bowl.
You didn't care that we were on the border.
The border of political pressure and oppression.
That socially, if either one of us got caught with the bowl
Or the feelings it could mean life.
Chased out with torches. Torture.
Secrecy was safer.
The community marked you *peligro* and I was in the public eye.
Every move I made was being watched.
The only time I got to touch you was on the back of your *moto*,
I remember pressing my chest to your back.
Hoping my heart seeped through the clothing
And you could feel my desire.
Almost got kicked out twice, so I laid low.
That didn't mean I didn't love you.
It meant I had to be strategic
To stay alive
You became a metaphor for happiness unattained.
A simile for a smile unseen. An emoji erased.

You became a stove, I wanted to be near the stove, to touch the stove,
Yet had to be conscious of heat and proximity.
So I didn't burn.
Your mom knew, she lectured us about the *Biblia*.
Pressured us to go to church for protection.
Protection.
Funny how fear makes us do things
Even as adults.
People in the town of 300 knew.
One day while I was teaching,
A 7-year-old student asked if I was a *lesbiana*.
I got scared. Really scared.
Terrified of my own heart beating me.
So I had to save us.
Made decisions to save us.
Slept with a guy to save us.
Hardest decision I ever made.
Everyone found out.
All of my problems went away.
You went away.
And no one questioned again.
Except me, I questioned.
Still question.
Every time someone said his name
I would think and question.
Kati, Kati Liliana Gatgens.
you called me Christine
But I always felt like an Adam and you,
You always felt like an Eve.
Te quiero.

To Kiss Her

Is such a rarity, involves more diamonds than gold can hold.
It's like being on a plane in 3-Dimensions with so much turbulence,
You're not sure when and if it'll land.
It's never-ending pillow fights with soft lips and feather tips,
A thumb war that never quite gets to ten.
1,2,3,4,5,6,7,8,9—let's start again.
To kiss her
Is a wrestling match I'll never tap out of and no one wants to win.
It's a sunny day in the middle of a blizzard, it's desert storm
mixed with hurricanes and icebergs.
Everything and nothing, doesn't even make sense.
To kiss her
Feels naturally like Fifty Shades of forest trees with hand grenades.
Where caterpillars turn to fireworks displays
And radios play morse code on repeat.
You'll try to stand as your knees take a seat
And morse code plays
Through soft lips and fingertips,
As fireworks burst
With pulled pins
Titanic sinks in quicksand
Nothing turns to everything
And turbulent winds count down from 9
As our plane starts to land
And you ask her…can we not count next time?

Revolving Compass

The moment a baby enters this world, they leave home.
Before being held in their mother's arms, umbilical cord is cut,
Severed from nutrients, taken from safety.
For some, a bond between mother and baby strengthens
As baby cries and mother consoles them, mimicking the womb.
For others, baby is taken away and becomes a lost soul.

I was 7 years old

When my umbilical cord was cut again and I entered foster care.
A place that had different meanings and definitions of home.
Depending on who you asked.
Sometimes it felt like there was never enough love.
Like screaming and manipulating for attention, just to be held.
Sometimes it felt like empty stomachs,
Walking the streets, watching families during mealtimes
And being hungry, for more than just food.
Most of the time it felt like my fault, my fault.
As earthquakes erupted on my insides—
Why does my mother ignore me? Why doesn't my daddy call me?
Where is our connection? I didn't understand.
We didn't understand.

So we settled for temporary.
Temporary food found in Lunchable containers,
Temporary love found in the handouts of strangers,
Temporary family found in anyone who felt sorry enough,
Temporary homes with temporary people and temporary care
Until even temporary wasn't there.
And I was still lost, abandoned file in forgotten storage bins
Lost in paperwork, lost in a sea of names.
But as I grew older, I started to find myself.

Began to understand my own GPS and navigate.
Learned how to love myself,
It wasn't too late, it's never too late but it could start sooner.
Temporary hands can be a compass directing to our own heart,
Show us how to identify, honor and regulate emotions,
Love holistically, the physical skin and person within
As the world will tell us.

How to hate ourselves.
Discriminate ourselves.
Be ashamed of ourselves.

So hold us and teach us how to hold ourselves too.
Temporary hearts can show us that there is one heart that stays forever.
And foster care and self-love into our soul.
And foster care and breathe peace into our soul.
You can't be the forever home, no one can promise the womb,
But you can show us the value of our own vessel.
And help guide our soul whole.
And help guide our soul home.

V. SHADOW SELF

Formidable Shadows

We talk about the parts of a plant
                      But hardly mention the
                                shadows

The underside of each leaf
        What lingers at the bottom of the soil
                What about the places where the sun never touches
                          Never reaches?

I googled it one day
        And learned—the less light received
                The less food produced
                        The plant then kills off parts of itself
                            Not receiving enough rays
I wonder how the plant knows
        Does it go by size?
                The larger the leaf the more it can absorb
        Does it go by color?
                The darker the green the more nutritious
        Does it go by sound?
                Can it hear the whispers of other leaves in the wind?

I wonder about my own shadows
        Can I ever see them if the light never reaches?
How do I cut off a shadow I cannot see?
      Do I go by size?
      Do I go by color?
      Do I go by sound?
    For now, I close my eyes and form.

PTSD Love

Insomnia attacks me at night…twisting around my limbs, I breathe it in…choke and gag.

Tears frozen in tear ducts. I wish they'd thaw. But they started freezing before my heart did and if you know anything about Michigan, even when the sun's out, you still see your breath.

It all started with a nightmare, while I was awake.
Maybe I can't sleep because I miss my comforter, the one with arms that wrapped around me gently each night…or maybe I can't sleep because my comforter turned cold and left me solo, sometimes even stabbing me in the back before leaving me, wounded to fend off frostbite by myself. His hips remind me of tribal dances and rituals that slowly became tedious traditions… His lips still give me shivers turned to slivers and shivs down my spine.

I should go to a chiropractor, get a dose of hands touching me, at least these aren't filled with empty promises and always waving goodbyes. Chiropractor's hands are guaranteed relief.

He had insomnia…ironically…he gave it to me.
Along with PTSD.

For a moment. I remember sometimes he touched me so sincerely I thought we were the last line in a letter before we wrote our names, together, shivering, not from the pain, or the cold, but mutual ecstasy.

Other times we were nose kisses, healing hugs and whispers of I love you and you're beautiful. Beauty is in the eye of the beholder, and you held me, with your gaze.

Telling me to walk this way and to say your name.
AJ
You gave me PTSD Love.

We had 12 years of torrential hurricanes and 70-degree perfect skies.

Now when I think of you, I see a villain. I see roadkill that won't fully rot away. I feel insomnia, frozen tear ducts, choking, gagging. I need a cigarette, to keep me breathing. PTSD Love

I am Permanently in Foster Care

Continuously filling bags to carry from place to place
never really finding a home.

Misplaced. Lost. Not Found.

Even as an adult.

I am a Temporary Home

A foster kid fighting for affirmation, love and affection.
I am affirmation, love and affection.
I am keeping the peace, solving everyone's issues and living as toxicity.
I am the peace, I am my own solution and I am the antidote.
I am sabotaging my own self, creating chaos and self-blame.
I am healing, communicating with expression, and creating safe spaces.
I am lost memories, trauma bonded and people pleasing.
I am living in the present, creating new memories
and boundaries with nurturing connections.
I am drama and I am broken shells.
I am interrupting repeated cycles
and building sandcastles from broken shells.
I am self-love and smiles.
I am scared and I am crying, depressed and anxious.
I am breathing, I am breathing
through the fear and naming all of the emotions.
I am running, I am distancing,
I am creating more barriers and walls.
I am a bridge, I am constructing safely.
I am safe, I am safety, I navigated safely.
I am reliable, I am trustworthy, I can trust me.
I can trust me
Trust me
I can trust me.
I am my permanent home.

Effervescent

To the girl I used to know
To the girl I used to be
The one who wore make-up to cover insecurity
High heels and skirts to mask low self-esteem
She had the largest hoop earrings, lassoing the senior boys and jealous girls
To that girl, the girl that lived in that dichotomy, that binary
Who looked in the mirror and pinched her stomach in envy

To the girl who over exercised and played gym for fun
Who did track, volleyball, competitive cheer, cross country
And never thought she was enough
To the girl who took the painful words of others
And carved jack-o'-lanterns into her vessel
The insults marking her to prove
She could take the pain and wear it as armor
The girl who got called a slut and went mute
Made herself invisible, shadowing the mice

You were among average and you were beyond average
To the girl who let people use her and touch her
She wanted to feel wanted
And never felt wanted
To the girl who cried herself to sleep next to a boy who didn't care or comfort

To the girl who ran away
whose legs turned to quicksand
To the girl who drank too much and let strangers slide
Their fingers in her throat
Too drunk to give a damn

To the girl who overachieved and overcompensated
With recognition and all A's
Who got lost in needing approval
Who wanted validation
The girl who chased the boys but wanted the girls

To the girl I used to know
To the girl I used to be
I'm so glad you're finally letting go
And you're growing into me.

Coming Out

You see me but only the outside
and preconceived notions cloud your judgment of my reality.
I'm not trying to hide…I just haven't come out to you.
You may not understand why I get so frustrated when you say
illegal immigrant or when you justify with religion.
You see, I haven't told you how I came from immigrants and how
my uncle committed your biggest sin…suicide.
And me, my abortion decision.
I haven't told you why I care so much about the rights of the
LGBTQ and equality,
because my gender and sexuality are on a continuum, and I cannot
deny my thoughts, feelings and emotions.
I haven't come out to you about how I grew up in poverty and how
I used education to conform and rise above this generational cycle,
trying to not become part of the 96% who get stuck.
I haven't told you how my perceived gender affects me on the daily
and how I've internalized racist comments
and feel ashamed every time I walk into a room.
Not just any room but one with heavy air feeding the systems of
oppression that keep my voice from being heard.
I haven't come out to you about my hunger…my hunger for
not just food that I can't afford but for systematic change.
My desire to not be left in the cycle of poverty
that statistics has destined me for.
Another female, Latine, a victim, statistically poor…
I haven't come out to you
but I'm coming out today.
La lucha sigue…
The fight continues.

Metaverse Brain

I'm 31 years old and self-diagnosed with ADHD and autism
like I've been living with my brain now for a minute
and started noticing my superpowers.
Such as the ability to talk to you about the process of
metamorphosis, listen to my inner monologue before I speak
and notice that your shoes are untied, the teapot is ready
and the toilet squeaks when no one is using it.
That's pretty damn impressive.

I've learned I need to script as scripting keeps my brain on task
and increases communication and predictability—
leaving everyone calmer and quenching any anxiety in the room.
My social anxiety at times keeps me listening to conversations
and people feel heard and seen.
I follow the dopamine—so if it doesn't feel right it quickly goes out
of my radar—ridding myself of toxicity and only keeping the pure.

I can hyperfocus on tasks for hours or procrastinate till 20 minutes
before the deadline and still get it done—sometimes.
And I am the main character,
the superhero, creating my red-carpet journey.
I've met other superheroes along the way
Like dyslexia who thinks in 3D images
and creates visuals naturally with their mind.

My ADHD also comes with a reset button called depression that
activates when I am needing deep rest for my mind and soul—
allowing it to reconnect and recalibrate with my body.
It also has a fast-forward button called anxiety
that allows me to speed ahead to what ifs and possibilities.
The one thing I've never honed is my ability to control the buttons.
And take them off automatic.

Ventriloquist Song

Hierarchical hands / grip at my sides
leading me to dance / in their rhythm
      Their beat

I am a puppet
Ventriloquist singing in their choir
I am a sold-out concert during COVID
Everyone has tickets to the show
But nobody feels safe enough to go
And no one wants to be there

Hierarchical hands / replace my own
As prosthetic / mechanic

With the same body, I no longer have control
Never studied robotics but understand how machines work
How systems maintain
Hierarchical hands grease the parts that are making too much noise
So the squeaking stops and the machine stays in its rhythm
And I am two left feet dancing
To the chorus on repeat
Feeling defeated

But hierarchical hands with enough pressure
Can soften their grip
We will mold the clay through community
And sway the machine
Dance to our own step, our own rhythm
Magnetized by conscious decisions
To get back to nature and our roots
With equity inclusion and justice
So we're united
              as stated in our name.

1000 Photographs

"How are we getting in?"
She looked at me in excitement.
"Just follow me. Play follow the leader."
I looked at her as a liability.

As we rushed to the front of the line
Analyzing, observing, watching.
I understood humans.
Their movement.
Trained my whole life for this.
I knew how to not be seen.
Be unheard.
Unnoticed.
Dust in the dark.
"Ticket please," the attendant motioned me
to a group searching for their right to be there.
My green card.
I analyzed, no one was watching.
I observed the flow of the crowd.

Blended in like spider webs in the corner of a room,
Liability behind me.
I camouflaged successfully.
Felt like the coyote.
Got past security checkpoint one.
Next up, metal detector.
No weapons, no money and no keys.
Definition of rural poverty, me.
Passed.
Wouldn't if I were the coyote.
Security checkpoint three ahead.
He looked busy,

Hardly able to catch his breath.
I'll make it easy.
Flashed my phone
So fast.
His crepuscular eyes of a deer.
Afraid to get hit with my confidence.
Gave me permission.
I was in.
Looked behind.
Liability was in too.
On the wind of white privilege.
And my confidence.
We looked up at the snipers
Pointed in another direction
At a browner coyote and their pack.
Obama on the podium,
Bernie right beside.
I had every right to be there,
So many others never made it.
Deported by the promised land
By this man,
And me sneaking past snipers to see his speech.
The disconnect, the injustice.
When words don't match actions.
All you have is 1000 pictures
With no meaning or definition,
So through tears I started recording.
Snapped a few.
Was it worth it?
I guess the grass is greener
On the other side of the lens.
Because it's fake and filtered.
No water needed.

Orlando

Run, queer girl, run. The system was not made for you and to be welcomed, you must run from who you are. Hide away those vibrant colors that make you unique.

Run, gay boy, run. Socially, you'll be oversexualized or demonized as HIV, your penis being envied and stripped from your body. Them taking away your true value and off-branding it.

Run, queer, run. You will gain rights but then be fired and legally discriminated against…you're not worth their value…they don't value your true worth.

Run, trans girl. Run, trans boy. They're afraid of you using their restrooms when you should be afraid—as real predators get a warning sentence and second chances.

Run, human, run. They've commercialized your identity, mascotted your colors and made a profit from your celebration.

Run, gender non-binary, non-conforming. Because they demand you to have a label but then cringe and over ask for explanation.

Run cuz they're shooting words, run cuz they're firing spit.

Run cuz they're shooting bullets, they're firing bullets, actual bullets, forcing you into the bathrooms they banned you from.

Run cuz they're chasing you with their ignorance and they're tagging your life in a hashtag line.

Run, Latinx, run. They don't understand the x, don't know that binary gender is inherent in your language and you can't get away. So you x it out.

Run, Hispanic, run cuz they're inviting you to work and then scream illegal while dropping you off to a place you never came from.

Run, Chicanx, run from the green that the American Dream promised you while asking for your green papers and taking your money.

Run, Muslim, run. They're judging you, they're blaming your kindness as you live love—

Run, Islam, run. They're shaming your name, they're tainting your religion and painting it in blood.

Run, beautiful, run because in the same line they condemn your identity they claim you and pray while using your pain to further their agenda.

Run where you are free to be as you desire…where no chains squander your accomplishments.

Run, my child, run because you're not welcomed, only the guns are.

Run till you don't have to run anymore

Cuz you're home.

Coworker

This man, a stranger at best, became best friend at most.
He says he's grateful for my existence.
I ask to repeat again
As no one has ever said that
In those words.
And he repeats every time at lunch.
Doesn't know how much I need to hear
Someone is grateful that I exist.
      The one thing I've never wanted to do.
           Exist.

Singed Piña

There were only three in the field that day.
On July 21st, 2018.
Three.
Digging the trenches.
When it happened.
The town says he was listening to music.
They say he had his phone in his hat.
Headphones dancing to the beat of his eardrums
When without warning,

Lightning struck.

The air was dry.
The sky blankly staring.
They say it was an act of God.
That he was in the path of wrath.
The two survivors disagree.
Burnt pineapple singes their tongues.
Is it worth coming to work tomorrow?
For less than two dollars an hour?
Is there any other option?

Sin documentos, sin papeles.

Dulled machetes on their hips swinging as the bosses
Right the obituary.
And all the blaming commences.
No cellphones allowed in the fields
He knew that.
Mandatory CPR classes
He'll be another
Quick lawsuit
Get a Good Lawyer.

And then…

His employers will forget his name
His tombstone will be blank if he has one at all
His coworkers will deliver the body
His mother will phoenix cry amongst the ashes
His brothers will have no other choice and return to the trenches.
His sister will pray on each rosary bone.
His father, well he's going to meet him again soon
And complete the generational cycle
Employers will talk about safety for a while,

Apologize

Then everything will go back
To daily routine.
Back to normal.
But not for his family.
Normal will be
Whited-out
from
their
vocabulary.

2021 Masquerade

In a small town where everyone knows each other and funeral is at the same church every year,

I've memorized the pews, the processions, the people. A repeat haunting of past and present…souls.
We've been through this graveyard before.

The tombstones are a phone book that no one reads anymore, 4 years ago and 3 years ago and 1 year ago, last month and now. We don't know it yet, but in 3 weeks as well, I start to wonder,
Am I the one haunting the dead?
Am I the ghost disturbing the peace?
My niece has a pre-packed bag for funerals.
She carries it expectantly,
accustomed to death lurking around every coroner.
I shiver.

The drive is familiar, robotic. I've learned the radio station knobs like how I've memorized the time.
As a machine that I wish to climb into. I'm in…
the middle of this town of 4,000 and the only radio station is a fuzzy Christian channel. I usually change the station relentlessly but not today. It stays, fuzzy like my insides.

I walk these aisles, kneel at these pews—a choreographed remorse. I can cry on cue, my eyeballs are black and etched with the number 8. I call the pocket and use my tears as pool sticks to shoot my grief into the hollows of my heart.
To bury in each ventricle until
I'm numb.
Novocaine can't hide the pain of grief
you never learned to deal with.

There's windmills everywhere along the drive and they're slicing the air like raw steak. I can feel it in my chest. The wind cutting into my throat and landing on each ventricle.

I pull up to the church at 9:27 am, 3 minutes early.
I almost take a break before entering but the church bells start ringing and I must run to make it on time.
I cannot be late to someone else's funeral, only mine.
Familiar figures I haven't seen in years, greet with piercing glares.

The procession begins and we all go through the routine. The wine tastes like the blood from that raw steak. The awkward stranger next to me asks what the smell is and I realize the stranger is my ex's new girlfriend. I plug my nose.

We walk outside, get in our cars and follow the hearse to the hole.
The hole where we will bury the smell and pieces of every heart.
Everyone is quiet as the casket lowers.
Everyone except my 3-year-old niece who keeps asking her daddy, what happened?
Daddy what happened?
And he answers with a shhh—
And tells her to keep her mask on.

Cortisol Addiction

Love is painful and leaves scars,
The regular cliché.
Boo, you were no cliché.
With 19 face piercings,
Lost count of your tattoos.
I couldn't catch myself from wanting your lips
That were more dagger than pillow.
Your heart, more metal cage than teddy bear.
And I was addicted to pain.
Literally, my brain grew up on cortisol.
I saw every red flag as green.
The bull inside rushing toward you.
My red flag, my matador.
A cliché I never got to say.
We were always repelling.
Too afraid to touch.
One of us always pulled away
Before contact.
Afraid to tear the flags in shreds.
To spew threads,
So I kept you at a distance.
Stayed six feet from your heart.
Every time we hugged, I kept my mask on.
Just in case, for safety.
We could blame it on COVID.
We both know the only positive was our inability to love.

Nightmares
A response to teaching as an English Interventionist

You screamed "Thieves—you are stealing," to students who
already felt unworthy. Your anger bouncing through their ears and
settling in their hearts.
The pain noticeable on their faces as one said,
"We are not the thieves."
Defiance in her eyes saying "we have every right to be here, your
people stole this land anyways."
You blame their culture for any behavior
that doesn't fit in your category of civilized.
Hard working Americans?
Please, I bet they've worked harder
and are more adult than most adults here.
You need to learn to speak English because the official language
of the United States is, oh shit. We don't have one. But we do
have many languages spoken and once you get past the genocidal
murder that happened, I guess you could say we were founded by
immigrants in a fucked up sort of way.
The ignorance in your voice disgusts me
and you don't quite understand a refugee's story.
So I'll tell you one.

She's having nightmares again, rolling around in her sleep.
Can't seem to wake up from her terrible dreams.
You see these aren't just nightmares that she has once in a while,
these are her life.
Flashbacks to her past that enter her brain every night,
causing the deepest explosions and volcanic ruptures mixed
with tornadoes and hurricanes spinning her around and around
until...she wakes.
Tears in her eyes, she realizes it was just a dream
but it felt so real—as real as her vivid memories.

A flashback to when she was 8 years old and met that stupid
pendejo who wouldn't take no for an answer.
As he trapped her in his bedroom.
Another night she dreamt she was back in Honduras
planning on running away when a neighbor kid told.
I'm sure you could guess what happened next.
She rubs the scars to numb her memory.
The life of a refugee.
She did eventually make it but walked 8 days and nights alone to
Mexico until she could find the right time to cross into freedom.
Her new life would soon be happening.
The life of a refugee.
See, this story is about a hero I met not too long ago,
a child with more wisdom than eyes could see.
To some she seemed too happy, too quiet, too bold.
But let me tell you how her story unfolds.
She came to the U.S. seeking a better life but was detained when
crossing the border. In a holding cell she was interrogated to tears
and treated like a criminal. She was 15. Her cellmate was 10 and
their brother hadn't made it.
Finally, she was deemed as lucky to be set free as a refugee but
it wasn't that easy. She was sent up north and lived at an all
Christian residential home.
Placed in a school where she had no idea what people were saying.
Forced to adapt without any family…
The life of a refugee. Screaming for her mom, cutting for answers.
And living in her nightmares each night.
I wish I could tell a good ending to the story but all I know is
that she's still surviving and needing a mentor like you to guide
your heart to hers and support her through her past and present
nightmares.

Water is a Universal Language
Recited at the Climate March on October 23, 2021

Lios em chaniavu—esta frase es indigena, es de mi tribu, Yaome/Yaqui, de Sonora, México

Soy indígena soy mexicana y he estado dos veces colonizada. Uno en inglés, el otro en español. Y todavía estoy aquí.

I'm here as another body of water.
Growing up on-and-off the Anishinaabek reservation
Unable to drink it.
I remember the do not drink posters
Climbing each letter after gym class
With my eyes—thirsty.
I remember the vacant air from the fountains
Too contaminated for consumption.
The Culligan jugs bubbling til the money ran dry.
I remember the desert of my throat
Swelling with spit
And finding refuge in Coca-Cola vending machines.
Our water was poisoned with PCBs,
Polychlorinated biphenyl.

¿Qué pasa cuando la tierra es robada por los colonizadores?
Colonized with capitalism
Lios em chaniavu, recuerdas?

When a town can't drink the water—
The grass turns brown on each side.
You lose count of funerals,
Death by suicide is normalized.
The fish disintegrate in your hands.

Most of your peers drop out
And quench their thirst with addiction.
Friends get airdropped to prison,
Women are not able to have children,
Children are not able to be children.

Now.
I work and live in Grand Rapids.
Water is plentiful
Around 240,000 bodies live here.
But if a mother cries in the 49507 does anyone hear?
What if she's Black or Brown?
As if her culture is just a color
In a crayon box—a piece of wax
To be used and discarded.

If she's crying is it too late?
Must she drink her own tears?

¿Qué pasa cuando la tierra es robada por los colonizadores?

Líos em chaniavu, líos en chaniavu
Recuerdas?

In 2016 news headlines read
"More children in 49507 than Flint poisoned by lead."
We were outraged,
But only for a minute.
So I ask again, if a Black or Brown mother cries in the middle of the city within the city, in this bubble—and it's not at a commission hearing, is anyone listening?
Must she melt and make a mess
All over the parking ticket?
If she can only remember her color
Will anyone care?

How many tears does she need to drink?
Before awakening the Dead Sea?

We know the issues.
That's all we focus on.
Division is the fastest street in this city
When I got to Grand Rapids,
I was told to stay in my lane,
But my lane has always been burning.
And the grass was never green on any side.
I'm tired of working in silos.
City officials with bottled water.
We're in the same water cycle
Plaster Creek polluted since 1910,
Dumping into Lake Michigan.
Plastic won't protect you.
It's bottled from the same source,
Ask Nestlé.

La tierra me dio a la luz, nací de su lámpara
Su agua me limpia, sus semillas me sostienen.

A maple carries 100 gallons of water on its leaves after a storm.
We're in the storm,
Nature can hold us through.
Water is the source,
Water preserves us.
Mni Wiconi
Water is the creator.

Líos en chaniavu
Dios te preserva. ¿Recuerdas? ¿Recuerdas?
Water preserves you. Remember? Remember?

Rooted Canal

Ellos te robarán los dientes si los dejas. —Mi Abuelita

They'll rob your teeth if you let them
They being the dentist
The doctor
The pharmacist
The insurance company
Collection agents
The ones with good intentions
The saviors
They being the system
The patriots
The "woke"
The capitalists
Los güeros
Them we do not trust
Them we do not let in
We stand only by kin
We stand only by
Kin who stand by us
No matter how hard the hustle
We stay together
We build together
We survive together
We thrive together
If we divide
We are extracted
Tooth by tooth
Cada diente
Become tombstone
Until we're empty
    —they are reason cadavers don't get cavities.
They'll rob your teeth if you let them.

VI. EMBRACING THE LIGHT

Status 1

It's an interesting place to be, at peace—noticing every person as their character and role—their insecurities no longer your worries. The projections not causing pain. The fire alarm went off this morning and I kept cooking until it stopped. Unphased. Peace. ♥

Status 2

Do not expect the house to be built for you—you must build the home from within first.

Status 3

Slow down, breathe in this season. Hydration? Have you eaten? Did you smile, laugh or play today? How about sat down to reflect or pray? Slow down, what did you release to be more at peace?

Status 4

Be still my love and feel the wind caress your cheek, the grass massage your muscles and your entire body fertilize in the ☼ sun.

Status 5

Sometimes you have to leave roads unpaved and dirty. I've always tried my hardest even when it was sedimentary stone and falling apart.

Synchronized Divination

Divine timing matches the bird with the nest
Divine timing chooses the sizes of each twig
Divine timing finds the twine to tie faulty fragments and loose ends
Divine timing brings the lost lover to share the treasures
Divine timing molds the tweets into lullaby and nursery rhyme
Divine timing holds the shells complete
Divine timing shells the complete while holding
Divine timing moves the nest to warmer sun
Divine timing breaks the twigs together
Divine timing flies to stronger posts
Divine timing nurtures new wings from broken shells
Divine timing feeds the fragile mouths with moving parts
Divine timing is thankful the nest of old is not the nest of now.

Utility Poles Stay Stagnant

Growing up I was told…you have so much potential. As an adult I've been sold as having so much potential. Potential meaning potent, meaning having or showing the capacity to become or develop into something in the future. Meaning not quite there yet. Lacking. Needing nutrition. Malnourished.

The irony of potential is that it's an energy and if energy is not in motion, it stays stagnant. Unable to move forward.

I grew up as a utility pole—a tree with no roots, my bark stripped of its culture, its language and identity removed, so I lived bare. Nude. No branches to lift me higher. No leaves to soak in any sun. So I kept sunscreen on.

Luckily Michigan is so cold. Not many warm hearts here. Michigan made us…made us assimilate—scrub off the dirt from our skin. Skin. *Piel*. Peel—that's all I ever wanted to do was peel. Mine. Off.

My grandma used to grab my arm, place it next to hers and say mija—I wish I had your skin. It's so beautiful. My life would be so much easier…if I had your skin.

Hers a darker utility pole—still with some bark and roots. Resembling the closest version of a tree—still living. Still nourished. Still. Stagnant.

I wonder where she would be if not sold the American Dream—or if she could've stayed in California with her cousins—she'd be such a magnificent tree, with all her rings, all her branches—living their highest potential.

Healing Cells

Each 7 years, every cell in your body is regenerated
and cells are the seeds we need to grow.
Even our bodies have a system of letting go.

You don't deserve to be lied to.
You don't deserve to be compromised.
A bruised fruit. Squeezed dry.

I'll repeat this to you over and over as a reminder.
Until it becomes a new cycle.
Please let it seep into your mind
and ignite love synapses onto each receptor.
Allow it to pump safety through your ventricles
and security into each vein.
You deserve so much. Just for being alive.

You deserve trust and love, communication and healing.
Balance and healthy connection.

I wish you confidence, self-realization, mindfulness, grounding,
physical emotional spiritual mental and intellectual health.

You were born to have profound roots,
pumping strength into your full heart.
You've been a walking wound for too long,
Still bleeding trauma from past lashes.

And they became repeated cycles, repeated relationships, repeated
actions, repeating beliefs that you are not good enough, that you
are not worthy, that you don't deserve.

But it's wrong. The trauma is wrong. Past cuts and wounds need to become scars and fade away.

Pour in the new and let go of old. Let fear become the catalyst, the bait to something better. Cast your line into the ocean until you find what you need. Mold the environment into your masterpiece.

I wish you peace, balance, beauty, purpose, hugs, so many hugs. Resilience, restoration, truth and honesty, connection, fun, intimacy, reciprocity and a life worth living,

Be-longing.

Be-long-ing

Longing to Be.

Illusion of Choice
A reclamation of self

It's interesting to say "my body, my choice,"
As I've never felt safe in mine.
I'm Yaqui native, born and raised
On and off the Anishinaabe reservation.
Reconnecting to my roots,
Finding safety in my body again,
While living in Grand Rapids Michigan.
Grand Rapids feels like Ursula.
Making deals here is signing your soul to the sea witch,
Except he's a man.
He'll take your voice and speak with it.

Here's my story:

I am a person
and I had an abortion
and kept it buried for years…
Now I'm digging up the burial of stigma
and opening the casket of shame to destroy it.
I had an abortion while driving and searching for a discreet place hidden from Google Maps.
I was alone, abandoned,
While protesters picketed their hatred and spit swords at me,
Stabbing the empty pit of sadness balled up inside my chest.
I had an abortion while millions have unplanned pregnancies due to rape, coercion and their business.
Searching for shiesty doctors because they have no other choice.
Mine was medically safe, medically sound
And my decision…
Decision: a conclusion or resolution reached after consideration.
A choice of free-will granted from Creator.

Policed by men.
1 in 4 pregnancies ended in abortion before Roe v. Wade.
1 in 4 pregnancies ended in abortion after Roe v. Wade.
This isn't about lowering numbers, it's another war on the poor.
69% support Roe v. Wade.
Many of the remaining 31 get paid by a for-profit prison complex.
Another way to displace the most vulnerable while saving face,
Making it harder to afford, then gentrifying some more.
I made $7,000 a year, my boyfriend who left… Made 10.
Being adopted from foster care, I knew the abuse there,
So I made a decision, after consideration.
I lost friends and family and gained a community.
Felt sadness and relief.
Alone and connected.
Multiple realities and truths.
Truth: the quality of being true, genuine, actual, or factual.
We each have our own.
And isn't the beauty of this nation that we get to choose our destiny?
If I asked each of you to draw a shape on a piece of paper,
You would each draw a different shape of different sizes.
If I said draw a square, each square would be unique.
If I said to draw a small square, they still would all be different.
Some would choose not to draw anything at all,
Others would rip up the paper and throw the marker on the ground.
None would be the same.
And you each got to choose your destiny.
If COVID taught us anything, it is how precious choice is,
Especially when it is taken from us.
I am a person and I am unburying my coffin…
No—demolishing my coffin of shame to tell you that I had an abortion and I am reclaiming myself.

Dissecting the Insect

My nickname for 10 years was cockroach.
Reasons being—I can survive anything.
My charm got people to feel sorry for me
And give me access to their love.
I learned how to please people
To get me things
And could survive the apocalypse
Off handouts and in-kind donations.
People thought I was doing them a favor
By taking their stuff.

Cockroach was meant to be an insult,
Something to keep me on the ground,
Unable to fly.
But with six legs and antennas that detect threats
In the air current,
I see you before you even know I'm a target.
Cockroaches feel their environment,
So work well under pressure
I've been burnt by the sun and still find peace in its heat.

We're faster than you think
A cockroach scatters at 3 miles per hour.
If they were the size of a human,
They would clock in at over 200lbs
I used to be so good at running,
Calculating 10 steps ahead.
Speaking of heads—cockroaches don't need them
Can live weeks without,
Living in their heart.

A 40-year Contract

Mom has had a 40-year contract with depression
Started at 16
Gorilla-glued to shadows
Unrecognized
Monsters in bed
Unseen
Listens to music
That brands bones
Depressed
Watches charcoal cauldron blazed
And wonders why
She's burning
Sees love
In familiar
In survival
A bright red kettle
Of hope stays at bedside
Collects dust
Unused
I watch
No longer afraid.

Imperfect Pictures

Why do we delete blurry photos? Hit the trash can when we see red eyes or an extra flab of skin? We should love mistook photographs. Undocumented moments. Moments that cannot be tamed by the lens. The blurry laugh line of your grandpa's smile as he sits back in his rocking chair telling stories of back in the day mischief and wandering. The camera knew that this moment was too great to be staged. The grasp of your mother's hand intertwined in yours as she takes her last breath. Tears uncaptured falling onto your hands. A child dancing in the wind, dandelion seeds swirling around, their laughter touching your cheek. Daring you to put down your phone and dance. Children are more knowledgeable than adults. They know that technology cannot replace interaction. They understand how to live life, to enjoy the sunrise, soak in the scents of flowers of grass and earth. Imperfect photos remind us that the screen cannot replace people. The night sky cannot be felt in a Facebook post. Dreams and aspirations will not be contained in 140 characters or a hashtag. Fears and regrets cannot fully be expressed or heard in a four-walled plexiglass solitary confinement. Love cannot be shared the same without the touch and hug of a friend. Active listening without distraction. Don't be mistaken, photographs are beautiful, we are able to capture a percentage of a moment through a mechanical apparatus that soaks in light…that is magnificent, but realize that there's always a place and time for everything. And though the camera can be an amazing tool, it can also be the knife that stabs us in the back as we lose moments with distraction. And if you must capture then don't pose, don't delete, post the photos with the least amount of preparation. The ones where you're extra hazy, laugh lines, wrinkles and too much makeup or too little. You never know when this moment will be captured and ruined.

Fell in Love with Perfect Imperfection

At a young age I learned to accept imperfection.
A crooked swing and broken crayons,
bent baseball bats and missing puzzle pieces.
I grew up with imperfection and it was perfect.
Slightly rotten fruit and flavorless ramen,
only cold water baths and rusting cars.
As a kid I was conditioned to live with imperfection,
to deal with imperfection, to be with imperfection.
Black and blue eyes, dodging angry shoes aimed at you,
lonely nights and tons of fights.
Alcohol cans scattered through the yard,
a drunk smell lingering throughout the house.
Hints of drugs in the bathroom
and teaching myself which substances were flammable
and testing to see how I could burn the pain away.
Searching for sobriety, someone with sobriety.
I learned that life consisted of
court cases, breathalyzers, hand oaths filled with lies.
New homes…new houses…families…strangers.
I prayed for perfection.
I prayed for my imperfection just being the leaky faucet,
slightly burnt toast and melted ice pops.
Soggy pasta and flavorless ramen and flickering light bulbs.
Dirty laundry and empty ice trays in the freezer…
Smelly socks and slightly rotten bananas.
Broken locks and soundless doorbell rings.
I kept praying.
As an adult I survived in imperfection.
A dollar in the bank account and bills barely paid,
fell in love with inconsistent education,
watched as he failed out of his dreams.
Watched him deal with addiction after addiction
that he couldn't afford.

I fell in love with his smile.
How he would help a wingless bird find a home.
He could make a trapped bumblebee feel safe.
I fell in love with his 3-string guitar under gray sunsets
and star filled night skies.
We were lazy kids.
Came from the same place,
an alcoholic mother and runaway/abusive dad.
He could make me laugh and he knew me inside and out.
We were poor but we were happy.
Now I smile reminiscing on those days.

Hiding Shadows

Recently I had a student, a teenager grab my wrist and point at the scars… She asked, *cortas también?*
And my heart sank like the Titanic but in a mosh pit.
Defenses rose up and concern.
I felt like I was in high school again trying to hide the fresh wounds with sweatshirts and still someone found out.
I was fresh-wounded and vulnerable again but this time I could embrace it and begin the healing of someone else's badgered arms.
So I said, *en el pasado* and *espero que pares pronto.*

Indisposable

I am not a disposable camera.
You cannot take pictures of parts of me
and throw the rest away.
I am colorful.
I destroy your images.
Distort your picture
and define me.

The Designer

They drew art on their skin with pen, markers, and razorblades, called it graffiti and watched the pain run down.
They make paper airplanes out of napkins, write hopes and dreams down and watch them fly through the window.

They dance to heartbeat, skipping through the lilacs.
They move to the wilderness, sway arms through the wind, feel hips shake like tectonic plates.
They exist.
Breathing, beating in art form.

The Shadow Waved and I Finally Recognized It

As friend

Not by color
Not by size
Not by the whispers of others
But by recognizing self
And the darkness I have held
How the light shines every morning
And the moon reflects every night
I recognized the wave as familiar
Someone I've known since first incarnation
But could not remember where we met

My shadow waved and I finally waved back
Recognizing how my existence is
Dependent on theirs
How the light does not exist without the shadow
How my shadow does not exist without my light
I saw the familiar cast of darkness
The lowering of self in shame
The insecurity
I smiled
Because we are one and I don't have to cut myself any longer.

Acknowledgments

I would like to acknowledge every soul that has been a part of my journey thus far and any future connections. Special shoutouts to my life-long friend, Kaylee Anderson, who has been with me through every phase of life. To my biological family who brought inspiration and found healing. My chosen families who took care of me. And open mics that helped cultivate my voice. Some of these open mics include the Drunken Retort in Grand Rapids, the Nuyorican Poets Café and all the open mics put on by the L.A. Poets Society. Also, this collection would not be possible without the intentional, inspirational and patient staff, teachers and mentors from the Community Literature Initiative, and specifically the National class. Some of the best teachers—Andy Sánchez, Anne Marie Wells, Marissa Forbes, Hiram Sims and of course my amazing classmates who have given me the best advice, critique and affirmation: Accountability partners—Jordyn, Marlana-Patrice, students from my first class: Neha, Estela, etc.

Next, I would love to acknowledge my creative team which includes editors, designers and collaborators.

Finally, I would like to acknowledge you, for believing in me and listening to a piece of my story.

[Note to Self]
You are dope as hell! The world needs to know, you need to share.
Love, this is bigger than you, remember you're (you are and your) WHY.
I know it's hard, anything worth anything is HARD. Imposter syndrome, procrastination and fear—CANNOT LIVE HERE!! Come on, you fucking got this. I believe in you, others believe in you. You got this. I promise this isn't the scariest shit you've done—this is just the testimony to some of the scariest shit you've been through. Repeat: I am a published poet. I sold out my first 1000 copies. Thank you universe. Asé.

www.ingramcontent.com/pod-product-compliance
Lightning Source LLC
Chambersburg PA
CBHW070150080526
44586CB00015B/1931